The Campus Cookbook
over 90 simple, tasty recipes

edited by David J Lock
and Hilary J Lotinga

Bath University Press 1980

ISBN 0 86197 024 1

Designed by Garry Denbury

Printed and published by The University of Bath
Claverton Down, Bath BA2 7AY

Contents

Introduction

The Campus Cookbook is for all those who want to prepare tasty and economical meals but who have limited experience of cooking, not much time, and only basic equipment. It has been compiled by students for students but is equally suitable for all those who find themselves in a similar situation.

The recipes have been graded by their degree of difficulty:

- for those who have never cooked before
- •• for those who are progressing
- ••• for those who want to be more adventurous

A list of suggested menus is included for those who like being prompted to cook something different. Notes on preparing vegetables, and when they are in season may also supply ideas.

All the recipes submitted by students have been successfully used by them, and with this assurance, but naturally disclaiming any responsibility for the end products, the editors wish you bon appétit.

David J. Lock
Hilary J. Lotinga

Notes

Imperial/Metric Conversions

Both metric and imperial measurements are given. Conversions may not always be directly equivalent because quantities have been calculated to maintain the basic proportions of the recipe. Either one, or other should be used throughout each recipe.

Frozen Foods

It is important that frozen meat, chicken, and fish should be thawed out thoroughly before it is cooked.

Pre-Heating the Oven

The oven should always be pre-heated to the specified temperature, before the raw ingredients are put in.

Oven Temperatures in the UK

In the UK at the present time (1980) electric ovens are marked in °F.

Abbreviations

The following abbreviations have been used:

tsp	teaspoon
tbsp	tablespoon
sp	spoon

Hints on Cooking

Vegetables
Vegetables provide a valuable source of vitamins, mineral salts and roughage, but their food value, appearance, and flavour can be spoiled by incorrect cooking. Buying, storage and preparation are also important.

Buying
Check that root vegetables are unblemished. In particular, avoid potatoes that are turning green. Any soil adhering to vegetables will help to protect them. Green vegetables should be a nice bright green—if the vegetables are at all yellow they are going stale and should be avoided.

Storing
If the vegetables are wrapped in plastic, unpack as soon as possible. Store the vegetables in a cool place out of direct sunlight so that air can circulate round them. Aim to use green vegetables within two days. Root vegetables may be kept longer.

Preparing
Green vegetables. Do not prepare the vegetables until just before cooking, as mineral salts will dissolve if they are soaked in water, and vitamin C will be destroyed if cut surfaces are left exposed to the air. Remove any imperfect outer leaves. Wash carefully in cold water.

cabbage	shred with a sharp knife
sprouts	cut a cross in the base of each sprout
cauliflower	trim the stem and green leaves, divide the head into florets
spinach	trim the stalks
broccoli	remove the outer leaves but leave flower heads and small leaves intact
beans	top and tail, remove any tough stringy edges, slice

Root vegetabes. Wash off excess soil, peel thinly or scrape the skin off young vegetables. New potatoes may be simply scrubbed. Cut potatoes into medium sized pieces or dice turnips, parsnips, or swedes, slice carrots. Wash in cold water.

oking

pare the vegetables. Put enough water into a saucepan to
e a depth of about 4 cms (1½ ins) for green vegetables, which
ok fairly quickly; 8 cms (3 ins) for root vegetables which take
ger.

Bring the water to the boil and add a good pinch of salt. When
water is boiling, add the vegetables steadily, not all at once,
that the water does not go off the boil. Cover and time the
oking.

Approximate timings (may vary according to size):

cabbage	3–5 minutes
sprouts	5–6 minutes
uliflower	10–12 minutes (may need about 6 cms (2 ins) water)
spinach	2–3 minutes (very little water needed)
broccoli	8–10 minutes
beans	4–5 minutes
potatoes	about 20 minutes
parsnips	20–25 minutes
swedes	20–25 mins
turnips	20–25 minutes
carrots	15–20 minutes (if sliced; 40–45 if left whole)

hen cooked, strain thoroughly, top with a knob of butter and if
ed a sprinkling of chopped fresh herbs, some freshly ground
ack pepper or a little grated cheese.

Cook Rice

ethod one: Use twice as much water as rice for quick cooking
e, or two-and-a-half times as much water for ordinary rice. Put
e rice, cold water and a good pinch of salt into a saucepan.
ing to the boil rapidly, stir, cover the pan and reduce the heat.
mmer for about 15 minutes, when the rice should be tender
d the liquid absorbed.

ethod two: Use about ten times as much water as rice. Bring
e water to the boil and add a good pinch of salt. Add the rice
hen the water is boiling, stir and cook uncovered for about 15
inutes or until rice is tender. Strain, and rinse with boiling water.

Pasta may also be cooked by this method. A little cooking oil
dded to the boiling water helps prevent the pasta sticking
gether.

Take care not to overcook rice or pasta. It is best served 'al
ente', that is when there is still a slight resistance in the centre.

Vegetable Seasons

	January	February	March	April	May	June	July	August	September	October	November	December
Broad beans						•	•	•				
French beans						•	•	•	•			
Runner beans							•	•	•	•		
Broccoli	•	•	•							•	•	•
Carrots	•	•	•	•	•	•	•	•	•	•	•	•
Celery	•	•							•	•	•	•
Corn on the cob								•	•			
Leeks	•	•	•	•						•	•	•
Parsnips	•	•	•	•						•	•	•
Peas						•	•	•				
Potatoes	•	•	•	•	•	•	•	•	•	•	•	•
Spinach			•	•	•	•	•	•	•	•	•	•
Sprouts	•	•	•							•	•	•

Frozen vegetables are available all the year round but are more expensive than fresh.

From *The Times Calendar Cookbook*
Katie Stewart
Hamlyn

Soups

● Leek and Potato Soup

serves 2

4 leeks
2 carrots
4 potatoes
parsley
chicken stock cube
575–870 ml (1–1½ pts) water
2 × 5 ml sp (2 tsp) cornflour
275 ml (½ pt) milk
salt and pepper
mixed herbs

1 Chop up leeks, carrots and potatoes in large chunks. Keep green pieces of leeks and chop up parsley.

2 Add 575–850 ml (1–1½ pts) chicken stock and simmer for 1–1½ hours, adding extra water if necessary.

3 Immediately prior to serving add green slices of leek, chopped parsley and cornflour mixed with milk. Add seasoning and mixed herbs. Cook until the soup thickens, then serve.

● Quick Onion Soup

serves 2

4 large onions
50 g (2 oz) margarine
875 ml (1½ pts) water
2 stock cubes (1 beef, 1 chicken)

1 Chop up onions, fry in margarine until brown.

2 Add 1½ pts of water and oxo cubes. Cook for 15 minutes. Delicious sprinkled with grated cheese and served with lots of toast.

● Vegetable Soup

serves 2

25 g (1 oz) butter
1 onion
selection of vegetables (potato, leeks, carrots, etc.)
1 × 15 ml spoon (1 tbsp) flour
425 ml (¾ pt) water
1 chicken stock cube
seasoning

1 Melt butter in a saucepan. Peel and chop onion and fry gently in butter until soft but not brown. Peel, wash and dice vegetables, add to onion and cook gently for 2–3 minutes.

2 Sprinkle flour on to vegetables, stirring to make a smooth paste. Dissolve stock cube in the boiling water and pour over vegetables, stirring all the time. Season to taste.

3 Bring to boil, stirring, and simmer for approx. 20 minutes or until vegetables are cooked and soup is thickened.

Note: "Starchy" root vegetables, i.e. potatoes, carrots, parsnips, etc., produce a thicker soup. Green vegetables, i.e. cabbage, sprouts, green peppers etc., make a lighter soup.

Mock Turtle Soup. Take 1 turtle, put in saucepan and proceed to mock it, saying 'now see how clever you are, get out of that!'

Snacks

• Quick "Pizza"

Toast a large slice of bread on one side only. Spread the other side with butter or margarine, then a thick layer of tomato purée. Sprinkle with oregano and cover with sliced or grated cheese. Grill until the cheese is melted and bubbling.

• Fruity Toast

Spread hot buttered toast with a little honey, top with mashed banana. Put under the grill for a few moments to warm the banana.

• Hawaii Toast

Put a slice of ham onto hot buttered toast, top with one pineapple ring, then cover with sliced or grated cheese. Grill until the cheese is melted and bubbling. Fill the hole in the middle of the pineapple with tomato ketchup or purée.

• Sunset Over Somerset

serves 1

2 slices of bread
French or German mustard
125 g (4 oz) grated cheese
butter or margarine
2 eggs

Spread the slices of bread with mustard (sparingly) and cover with the cheese. Put under a hot grill. When done, put a poached egg on the top of each piece. Serve hot.

● English Monkey

serves 1

1 large slice of bread
2 eggs
1 × 15 ml (1 tbsp) milk
salt and pepper
butter
50 g (2 oz) grated cheese

1 Toast bread.
2 Lightly beat eggs, milk and seasoning. Melt small amount of butter in pan, add egg mixture and scramble, adding cheese when eggs are about half cooked.
3 Serve on hot buttered toast.

• Wessex Quick Sauce for Chops, Liver, etc.

Use ½ packet of dried soup, make up into 8 fl oz with cold water and simmer for as long as packet says. The 'soup' should be nice and thick to make a tasty sauce.

Use vegetable soups with liver.

Use chicken soup with chicken joints.

Use lobster and shrimp soups with fish dishes.

• French Omelette with Herbs

serves 1

knob of butter or margarine
3 eggs
1 × 15 ml sp (1 tbsp) water
salt and pepper
large pinch of mixed herbs

1 Melt butter or margarine in omelette or frying pan. Mix eggs, water, seasoning and herbs together with fork, beating lightly.

2 When butter or margarine is hot put egg mixture in pan. Once mixture has begun to set, lift edges gently with a knife and tilt pan slightly, so that uncooked mixture runs onto bottom of pan and sets.

3 When omelette is set, fold in half and serve.

Variations: Alternative fillings may be added before folding, e.g. sliced or grated cheese, cooked chopped bacon, chopped ham, sliced cooked mushrooms, sliced tomatoes, sliced cooked onion and green pepper, sliced cooked potato, etc.

Cheese

- **Savoury Bread and Butter Pudding**

  serves 1

  oven temperature 180°C (350°F) gas mark 4

  2 slices bread and butter

  marmite

  125 g (4 oz) cheddar cheese (grated)

  150 ml (¼ pt) milk

  1 Place one slice of bread and butter spread with a little marmite in the bottom of a greased dish. Add a layer of cheese, the other slice of bread and butter spread with marmite and top with another layer of cheese.
  2 Beat egg into milk, add salt and pepper and pour over bread etc.
  3 Bake in preheated oven for 30–35 minutes.

- • **Pasta in Tomato Sauce**

  serves 1

  50 g (2 oz) pasta

  1 clove garlic

  1 × 15 ml sp (1 tbsp) tomato purée

  1 × 15 ml sp (1 tbsp) sugar

  1 pinch salt

  1 pinch pepper

  1 bay leaf

  mixed herbs

  1 Cook pasta shells, shapes, etc. as directed on the pack. (Usually involves boiling of 8–15 minutes).
  2 To make the tomato sauce, saute the crushed garlic clove in a little margarine in a saucepan. Add tomato purée and enough water to make a thick liquid. Add sugar, salt, pepper and herbs to taste. Simmer gently for 15 minutes adding a little water as necessary to keep sauce fluid.
  3 Strain pasta and stir into the tomato sauce to coat well. Serve on its own or on toast.

●● Crispy Cheese Pudding

serves 1

oven temperature 180°C (350°F) gas mark 4

60 g (2 oz) cheese
60 g (2 oz) white breadcrumbs
1 egg
150 ml (¼ pt) milk
¼ × 5 ml sp (¼ tsp) made mustard
salt and pepper

1 Grate the cheese and add to the crumbs. Separate the egg and add the yolk to the milk. Add the mustard, salt and pepper. Add this mixture to the cheese and crumbs and leave to soak for 20 minutes.

2 Whisk the egg white until stiff and fold into the cheese mixture.

3 Pour into a greased ovenproof dish and bake for about 40 minutes until firm and golden.

●● Cheese Risotto

serves 1

small onion
60 g (2 oz) mushrooms
butter
3 or 4 rashers of streaky bacon—diced
60 g (2 oz) rice
small tin peeled plum tomatoes
150 ml (¼ pt) chicken stock (chicken stock cube and 150 ml water)
seasoning
60 g (2 oz) cheese—grated

1 Chop onion and mushrooms and fry lightly in butter with the bacon (diced) until the onions are soft. Add the rice and fry for 1–2 minutes.

2 Add tomatoes and chicken stock and allow the mixture to simmer gently, until the rice is cooked.

3 Season to taste and add cheese, cooking the mixture until the cheese has melted.

Serve with a green vegetable of some sort.

••• Cheese, Bacon and Potato Hotpot

serves 4

oven temperature 200°C (400°F) gas mark 6

60 g (2 oz) butter or margarine
60 g (2 oz) flour
575 ml (1 pt) milk
salt and pepper
4 large onions
4 large potatoes
225 g (8 oz) bacon bits
125 g (4 oz) cheese

1 Heat the oven to 200°C. Make a white sauce by melting the fat in a saucepan, adding the flour and stirring to make a smooth paste. Then stir in the milk gradually and bring to the boil, stirring all the time, until thickened. Season and set aside.

2 Peel and slice the onions and potatoes. Remove the rind from the bacon and cut the rashers into small strips.

3 Grease an oven proof dish (with lid) and fill it with alternative layers of onions, potatoes and bacon. Grate the cheese and put three-quarters of it in the sauce which should be poured over the other ingredients, and sprinkle the rest over the top.

4 Cover the dish and bake for 1 hour. Reduce to 170°C (325°F) remove the lid and bake for a further hour.

Serve with a green vegetable.

Rabbit Fool. Take one rabbit, put in pan and tell it what a fool it is.

••• Quiche Lorraine

serves 4

oven temperature 200°C (400°F) gas mark 6

175 g (6 oz) shortcrust pastry (packet mix, frozen or home-made)
2 eggs
150 ml (¼ pt) milk
salt and pepper
3–4 rashers cooked, chopped bacon
50–75 g (2–3 oz) grated cheese

1 Use pastry to line a 20 cm (8 in) greased flan tin. Bake blind for 15 minutes. Lower oven temperature to 180°C (350°F) gas mark 4.

2 Meanwhile beat eggs, milk and seasoning together. Sprinkle bacon and cheese in pastry case, pour in egg mixture.

3 Bake for a further 30 minutes, or until filling is set.

May be eaten hot or cold.

Variations: Use chopped ham or chicken instead of bacon.

Use a mixture of cooked vegetables—sliced onions, mushrooms, potatoes, green pepper, peas, etc.

N.B. See 'Chicken Pie' recipe for home made pastry method.

●●● Pizza

serves 2

oven temperature 200°C (400°F) gas mark 6

half of 283 g (10 oz) packet bread mix (white or brown)
1 onion
1 clove garlic
butter or oil for frying
1 tin tomatoes
salt and pepper
oregano
1 green pepper
125 g (4 oz) mushrooms
175 g (6 oz) cheese

1 Make up the bread mix according to the directions on the packet. Leave to rise for about 1 hour. Knead thoroughly then divide in two. Roll each half into a ball, then flatten with the palm of the hand or a rolling pin to make a flat base. Lay on a greased baking tray.

2 While the dough is rising, prepare the tomato sauce. Peel and chop the onion, peel and crush the garlic. Heat the butter or oil in a pan and gently fry the onion and garlic until soft, but not brown. Add the tomatoes and their juice, season and add a pinch of oregano. Simmer until the sauce has reduced and thickened. Allow to cool.

3 Top each base with the tomato sauce. Remove the seeds from the pepper and slice the flesh thinly. Wash or peel the mushrooms and slice. Arrange the mushrooms and pepper on top of the tomato sauce. Sprinkle with the grated cheese.

4 Bake in the oven for about 20 minutes or until the filling is cooked and the crust is golden.

Variations: Ham, olives, anchovy fillets etc. may also be added.

Vegetables

● **Celery and Apple**

serves 2

celery
oil
2 cooking apples
2 × 15 ml sp (2 tbsp) soured cream
garlic salt
salt

1 Chop some celery into smallish pieces, fry it in oil, add the cooking apples (peeled and chopped), pour the soured cream over it and add garlic salt and ordinary salt.

2 Cook for about 20–25 minutes.

This is one way of serving celery hot and yet also very crisp. It can also be served cold as a salad.

N.B. Soured cream can be made by adding ½ × 15 ml sp (½ tbsp) of lemon juice to 2 × 15 ml sp (2 tbsp) of double cream, and beating until it thickens.

Irish Stew. Take Irishman and stew him.

● **Cole Slaw**

Quantities of vegetables according to taste.

white cabbage
carrot
onion
mayonnaise
lemon juice
salt and pepper

1 Shred the cabbage, peel and chop the onion finely, peel and grate the carrot.
2 Blend together with the mayonnaise, a little lemon juice and season to taste.

Additional ingredients may be added as desired, e.g. sliced celery, diced green pepper, cooked and cooled (or tinned) sweetcorn, sultanas, peeled and chopped apples, etc.

Alternatively mix the ingredients together with French Dressing.

French Dressing

salt and pepper
$1/4 \times 5$ ml sp ($1/4$ tsp) dry mustard powder
pinch sugar
2×15 ml sp (2 tbsp) vinegar
6×15 ml sp (6 tbsp) salad oil

Place all the ingredients in a screw-top jar and shake well until blended. Store in the fridge and use as required. Do not add to salads until just before serving.

•• Stuffed Potatoes

serves 2

oven temperature 180°C (350°F) gas mark 4

2 large potatoes
knob of butter
little milk
salt and pepper
50 g (2 oz) grated cheese
2 rashers bacon

1 Bake the potatoes for 1½ hours or until soft.

2 Cut in half lengthways and carefully scoop out the insides into a bowl. Mash with butter, milk and seasoning to taste. Mix in grated cheese.

3 Fill the potato skins with mixture, return to the oven for 5–10 minutes to reheat.

4 Top with freshly grilled or fried bacon.

Variations

Corn and Cheese: Mash the potato with butter, a little yoghurt and seasoning. Add 50 g (2 oz) grated cheese. Top with cooked or canned sweetcorn and reheat.

Soured Cream and Chives: Mash potatoes with butter, soured cream and seasoning. Add 1 × 15 ml sp (1 tbsp) chopped chives. Reheat.

Tuna and Tomato: Mash potatoes with butter, milk and seasoning (not too much salt). Mix with drained tinned tuna *sh. Top with sliced tomatoes. Reheat.

Farmhouse Potatoes: Mash potatoes with butter, milk and seasoning. Add sliced cooked mushrooms and sliced tomatoes. Reheat. Just before serving top with a spoonful of cottage cheese, cream cheese or freshly cooked scrambled egg.

●● Marrow Casserole

serves 2

oven temperature 190°C (375°F) gas mark 5

1 marrow (about 450 g (1 lb)
4 tomatoes
125 g (4 oz) grated or sliced cheese
salt and pepper

1 Peel the marrow, cut into 1 cm (½ in) slices and remove centre section containing seeds. Cook for 2–3 minutes in boiling salted water. Drain.
2 Arrange layers of marrow, sliced tomato and cheese in an oven-proof dish, ending with a layer of cheese, and lightly seasoning each layer.
3 Bake in the oven for 30 minutes, or until the marrow is soft and the top is nicely browned.

●● Vegetable Rissoles

serves 2

2 parsnips (or swedes)
2 carrots
2 potatoes
1 onion
25 g (1 oz) butter
1 × 15 ml sp (1 tbsp) flour
salt and pepper
pinch of thyme
25 g (1 oz) breadcrumbs
butter or oil for frying

1 Peel parsnips, carrots and potatoes, chop into fairly small pieces, and cook in salted boiling water for approx 15 minutes or until soft.
2 Peel and chop onion finely, add to vegetables with the butter and flour, and mash until smooth. Add seasoning and thyme. Allow to cool.
3 Form the mixture into balls, roll in breadcrumbs. Heat the butter or oil in a frying pan, and fry over a medium heat until the rissoles are brown on all sides.

Serve as a vegetable to accompany cold meat or fish.

Add peanuts to the mixture before forming into balls to make a vegetarian main dish.

●● Ladies Cabbage

serves 3

oven temperature 190°C (375°F) gas mark 5

1 small white cabbage
2 eggs
60 g (2 oz) melted butter
3 × 15 ml sp (3 tbsp) top of milk
salt and pepper

1 Cut up the cabbage roughly and boil in salted water for 15 minutes. Drain well and put aside until cold.

2 Heat the oven to 190°C. Chop the cabbage finely and add the beaten eggs, butter, milk, salt and pepper. Stir well and put into a buttered oven proof dish. Bake for 20–30 minutes until golden brown.
Grated cheese can also be added.
Can be eaten with meat and potatoes.

●● Vegetable Rissotto

serves 2

1 onion
4 large mushrooms
1 small pepper
butter for frying
175 g (6 oz) long grain rice (preferably brown rice)
1 tin tomatoes
tomato purée
salt and pepper
caraway seeds (optional)
1 small packet salted peanuts

1 Chop onion, mushroom and pepper and fry gently for few mins. Add rice, tomatoes and their juice and tomato purée.

2 Add seasoning and caraway seeds if used. Mix well and stir until mixture begins to boil.

3 Simmer for 25 minutes if using brown rice, 15 minutes if using white rice, or until rice is cooked. If mixture becomes too dry, add more water.

4 Just before serving, stir in peanuts. Alternatively use peanuts as garnish.

•• Curry in a Hurry

serves 2

25 g (1 oz) butter or margarine
1 onion, peeled and sliced
1 apple, peeled and chopped
1 × 5 ml sp (1 tsp) curry powder
1–2 × 5 ml sp (½ tsp) curry paste
25 g (1 oz) flour
275 ml (½ pt) water
1 × 5 ml sp (1 tsp) apricot jam
good dash soy sauce
diced fresh or cooked veg (potatoes, carrots, swedes, etc.)

1 Melt butter or margarine in pan, add onion and apple, and fry gently until soft.

2 Add curry powder, paste and flour, and cook for a few seconds. Remove pan from heat, add water (stock could also be used), vegetables, apricot jam and soy sauce and stir thoroughly. Return to heat and bring to the boil.

3 Add vegetables and lower heat. Cover and simmer for 20 minutes if using cooked vegetables, 40 minutes if using raw vegetables.

Serve with rice.

●●● Vegetarian Curry

serves any number

carrots
mushrooms
cauliflower florets
few frozen peas
pepper (red or green)
potatoes
onions
fat for frying
plain flour
curry powder
tinned tomatoes
seasoning
30 g (1 oz) long grain rice per person

1 Choose a number of vegetables from the list above.

2 Fry onion in fat and add vegetables other than peas, roughly chopped. Fry for about 5 mins.

3 Sprinkle with flour and add 1–3 × 5 ml sp (1–3 tsp) curry powder depending on taste, and tinned tomatoes.

4 Stir and simmer for 30 minutes covered with lid. Add extra water if necessary. Add seasoning. Add peas after 25 minutes.

Serve when all the vegetables are cooked.

Serve on long grain rice.

To flavour the rice and to add protein, add an egg to the rice once drained and returned to the saucepan, leave on the heat until the rice is completely coated with egg.

Fish

• Fish Provencale

serves 2

oven temperature 180°C (350°F) gas mark 4

25 g (1 oz) butter
2 fish steaks (fresh or frozen)
1 small onion
1 clove garlic
1 medium tin tomatoes
salt and pepper
mixed herbs or herbs to taste

1 Use butter to grease a casserole dish and place fish stakes in it. Peel and slice onion finely, peel and crush garlic and add both to fish.

2 Pour over tomatoes and their juice. Season and add herbs to taste (oregano is good with this dish).

3 Cook in oven for 30 minutes.

• Quick Fish Pie

serves 1

oven temperature 200°C (400°F) gas mark 6

1 small tin pilchards, sardines or tuna fish
salt and pepper
knob of butter
1 serving mashed potato (or make up instant)
25 g (1 oz) grated cheese (optional)

1 Mash fish (in sauce if there is one, but tuna fish must be drained). Put in greased dish and season.

2 Add butter to mashed potatoes and spread on top of fish. Bake in oven for 30 minutes.

3 Sprinkle cheese on top and brown under a hot grill.

• Quick Fish

serves 1

fillet smoked haddock 115–170 g (4–6 oz)
knob of margarine

Wash fish and place in cold water in frying pan. Bring to the boil and simmer for 20 minutes. Serve with a knob of margarine.

Goes well with fried or mashed potatoes and a green vegetable.

• Tuna Casserole

serves 3

oven temperature 170°C (325°F) gas mark 3

1 small onion
1 green pepper
small tin of evaporated milk
2 large eggs
200 g (7 oz) tin tuna fish
1 tin cream style sweetcorn or 1 tin creamed mushrooms
salt and pepper

1 Grate the onion and cut the pepper into small pieces. Beat the milk and eggs together in a large basin. Add the flaked tuna fish, sweetcorn or mushrooms, onion, green pepper and season well.

2 Pour the mixture into a well greased oven-proof dish. Bake uncovered for just under one hour.

This dish can be prepared in advance and kept in the fridge.

Fish Fingers. Take fingers off fish and cook them.

•• Eastwood Haddock

serves 2

45 g (1½ oz) butter
340 g (12 oz) haddock (or other white fish)
seasoning
1 small onion
small can tomatoes
1 bayleaf
mixed herbs
45 g (1½ oz) cheese

1 Melt 1 oz butter in a grill pan, cut the fish into two and lay in the grill pan. Add salt and pepper.
2 Chop and fry the onions in the remainder of the butter.
3 Drain the tomatoes and simmer with bayleaf, herbs and salt and pepper for 10 minutes.
4 When cooked, place the fish in a serving dish, cover with the sauce and sprinkle the grated cheese on the top.

Serve with potatoes and a green vegetable.

••• Mushroom and Fish Crisp

serves 2

oven temperature 180°C (350°F) gas mark 4

125 g (4 oz) spaghetti
60 g (2 oz) sliced blanched almonds
30 g (1 oz) butter
225 g (8 oz) cooked fish or 200 g (7 oz) tuna
85 g (3 oz) grated cheese
salt and pepper
425 g (15 oz) tin of cream of mushroom soup
1 packet potato crisps

Pre-heat the oven. Cook the spaghetti in boiling salted water for 12 minutes. Brown the almonds slowly in the butter, add the flaked fish, cheese, spaghetti and soup. Season and mix well and pour into a buttered casserole dish. Scatter the crushed potato crisps on the top and bake for 20–30 minutes.

••• Cod with Tomatoes and Anchovies

serves 2

oven temperature 200°C (400°F) gas mark 6

½ onion
1 large tomato
15 g (½ oz) tinned anchovies
1 green pepper
½ clove of garlic
1 × 15 ml sp (1 tbsp) olive oil
salt and pepper
2 × 150 g (5 oz) pieces of cod
45 g (1½ oz) tomato purée
little dry red wine

1 Pre-heat the oven. Slice the onion and tomato and cut the anchovies into small pieces. Remove the seeds from the pepper and slice thinly. Crush the garlic.

2 Place the oil, onion, green pepper and garlic in a saucepan and cook or 5–7 minutes stirring well. Add anchovies. Season.

3 Place half the mixture into a well greased oven-proof dish, cover with fish and place the rest of the mixture on the top. Arrange the tomatoes over the fish. Combine the tomato purée with the red wine and pour over the fish. Bake for 30 minutes, basting twice.

Serve with green vegetables and mashed potatoes.

Bloody Merry. ½ pt pernod and tomato sauce.

••• Tuna Macaroni

serves 3

125 g (4 oz) macaroni
30 g (1 oz) margarine
30 g (1 oz) flour
425 ml (¾ pt) milk
140 g (5 oz) cheese
200 g (7 oz) tin tuna fish
200 g (7 oz) sweetcorn
salt and pepper
60 g (2 oz) fresh breadcrumbs

1 Cook the macaroni in salted boiling water for 8 minutes, drain
  and rinse. Melt the margarine in a saucepan, add the flour and
  mix well. Add the milk a little at a time mixing well. Bring to the boil
  stirring all the time.
2 Add the grated cheese to the sauce and blend well. Add the
  macaroni, tuna and drained sweetcorn. Season well.
3 Heat the tuna macaroni gently and then turn into a hot oven-
  proof dish. Sprinkle the breadcrumbs over the mixture and put
  under the grill until they have browned.

••• Devilled Fish

serves 2

2 × 150 g (5 oz) pieces of white fish
150 ml (¼ pt) water
1 × 15 ml sp (1 tbsp) curry powder
15 g (½ oz) margarine
15 g (½ oz) plain flour
½ × 15 ml sp (½ tbsp) sweet pickle
lemon juice
salt and pepper
30 g (1 oz) breadcrumbs

1 Poach the fish in water for about 10 minutes. Remove the fish
  and flake, removing any bones.
2 Mix the curry powder with the water used for cooking the fish,
  making up to 275 ml (½ pt).
3 Melt margarine and stir in the flour. Add the curry powder mixture
  to make a sauce. Bring to the boil stirring well.
4 Remove from the heat and add the flaked fish, pickle, lemon
  juice and seasoning. Transfer to an oven proof casserole, scatter
  the top with breadcrumbs and either brown under a grill or heat in
  a moderate oven 170°C (325°F) gas mark 3.

Chicken

• Souped-up Chicken

serves 2

oven temperature 220°C (425°F) gas mark 7

2 chicken joints
25 g (1 oz) butter
salt and pepper
1 can soup (e.g. chicken, mushroom, vegetable, etc.)

1 Wash chicken joints, place in an ovenproof dish, dot with the butter and season.
2 Cook in oven for 30 minutes.
3 Pour soup over chicken and return to oven for further 15 minutes.

•• Simple Chicken Casserole

serves 1

oven temperature 190°C (375°F) gas mark 5

1 chicken portion
1 × 15 ml sp (1 tbsp) flour
salt and pepper
small amount of oil
1 small onion (chopped)
1 small can of condensed mushroom soup
½ can of water

1. Wash chicken portion. Mix the flour and salt and pepper. Coat the chicken with the seasoned flour (put the flour in a polythene bag with the chicken and toss).
2. Put a quantity of oil in a frying pan and add onion. Cook until transparent. Remove onion to a casserole dish.
3. Place chicken in the frying pan and cook quickly till just slightly brown on all sides. Remove to casserole.
4. Tip the remainder of the flour into the frying pan to absorb the chicken juices. Do not have the heat too high or the flour will burn. Cook for 1 minute and then add the soup and water, stirring so that the mixture does not become lumpy.
5. Pour into casserole dish. Cover and cook for 45 minutes to 1 hour.

Serve with potatoes and another vegetable.

•• Quick Chicken Pie

serves 4

oven temperature 200°C (400°F) gas mark 6

1 small onion
450 g (1 lb) cooked chicken portions
1 packet chicken noodle soup (1 pt packet)
450 g (1 lb) cooked potatoes
30 g (1 oz) butter

1. Chop chicken and onion finely and mix well.
2. Cook soup as directed on packet using only ½ pt water.
3. Mix chicken and onion with soup and put into a greased pie dish.
4. Mash potato and spread over the chicken mixture. Dot with butter. Bake in centre of oven for 25 minutes.

••• Chicken Pie

serves 2

oven temperature 220°C (425°F) gas mark 7

Pastry
125 g (4 oz) plain flour
pinch salt
60 g (2 oz) butter or margarine
1 × 15 ml sp (1 tbsp) cold water
or use 125 g (4 oz) shortcrust pastry mix

Filling
1 cooked chicken portion
25 g (1 oz) butter
1 × 15 ml sp (1 tbsp) flour
275 ml (½ pt) milk and water mixed
1 chicken stock cube
salt and pepper
1 onion
50 g (2 oz) mushrooms
few frozen peas
butter for frying

1 Seive the flour and salt into a bowl and rub in the fat with the fingertips until the mixture resembles fine breadcrumbs. Sprinkle on the water and blend, taking care not to over handle the mixture. Form the dough into a ball. Allow to rest in the fridge whilst making the filling.

2 Cut the chicken meat into small pieces. Melt the butter in a pan and add the flour, stirring to make a smooth paste. Carefully add the milk and water, and crumble in the stock cube, then bring to the boil, stirring all the time. Season.

3 Peel and chop the onion. Wash and slice the mushrooms. Heat the butter in a frying pan and gently fry the onion until soft but not brown. Add the mushrooms and peas and stir. Mix the chicken meat, vegetables and sauce together.

4 Roll out half the pastry on a lightly floured surface and use to line a greased 17 cm (7½ in) pie dish. Roll out the second half of the pastry. Fill the case with the chicken mixture, moisten the rim of the pastry with water and lay the pastry lid on top. Press the edges together and cut away the surplus pastry. Make a slit in the centre of the pie for steam to escape.

5 Bake for 30 minutes or until the pastry is cooked and golden.

●●● Chicken Corn Casserole

serves 2

oven temperature 180°C (350°F) gas mark 4

2 chicken joints
30 g (1 oz) butter
1 × 5 ml sp (1 tsp) oil
2 onions
60 g (2 oz) button mushrooms
seasoning
chicken stock cube (to make 425 ml (¾ pt) stock)
small can sweetcorn

1 Fry the chicken in the butter and oil until lightly brown, then put in the casserole.

2 Chop and fry the onions and put with the chicken. Add the mushrooms and salt and pepper.

3 Make up stock as directed on the packet and add to the casserole. Cook for 1 hour, adding the drained tin of sweetcorn after 50 minutes.

Serve with potatoes and one green vegetable.

Low Calorie Water Sorbet. Take 1 pt of water and freeze.

••• Chicken Casserole

serves 1

oven temperature 180°C (350°F) gas mark 4

1 chicken joint
30 g (1 oz) butter or margarine
1 medium-sized onion
1–2 cloves garlic (to taste)
½ rasher bacon (or end bits)
3–4 button mushrooms
chicken stock cube and hot water
salt and pepper
1 × 5 ml sp (1 tsp) herbs/bourquet garni
1 × 5 ml sp (1 tsp) cornflour

1 Wash the chicken joint and fry quickly on both sides in a saucepan in butter or margarine. The chicken should turn white to golden. When it is 'sealed', remove from pan. Fry chopped onions and garlic until golden then add bacon and mushrooms.

2 Put joint back into pan and pour on enough stock to cover the joint. Add salt, pepper and herbs to taste and simmer gently on stove for 45 minutes or until chicken is cooked. (Alternatively place in a casserole dish in a moderate oven for 1¼–1½ hours.) Thicken sauce as desired with cornflour mixed in cold water.

Serve with potatoes (boiled, roast, chips or jacket; bake especially if using oven anyway—takes 40–50 minutes for a medium–large potato), peas, sweetcorn, sprouts, etc.

Coq Au Vin
As above, but use 1 glass red wine in the stock and reduce amount of water.

Beef

- ## Braised Meat Slices

  serves 2

  oven temperature 220°C (425°F) gas mark 7

  2 slices of meat 125 g (4 oz) each

  425 ml (¾ pt) gravy (depending on the diameter of the dish)

  Wash the meat and lay in a casserole dish or sausepan. Cover with gravy, put lid on, and cook for 1 hour.

  Serve with boiled potatoes and any other vegetable.

- ## Maison Mince

  serves 4

  1 onion (chopped)

  450 g (1 lb) minced beef

  fat for frying

  1 green pepper (chopped)

  2 × 15 ml sp (2 tbsp) tomato ketchup

  1 × 15 ml sp (1 tbsp) tomato purée

  salt, pepper and a little stock

  small tin baked beans

  Fry the onion and meat, then add all the ingredients except the beans. Simmer for 30 minutes then add the beans and heat thoroughly.

- ## Stewed Steak

  serves 2

  350 g (12 oz) stewing steak

  425 ml (¾ pt) gravy

  Wash the meat and cut into 2·5 cm (1 in) cubes, removing fat. Make up gravy as instructed by packet. Put both in a saucepan, bring to the boil and simmer for 2 hours, stirring occasionally.

  This makes a wholesome meal with potatoes and one other vegetable.

  Can be re-heated by adding extra gravy and will be even more tender second time round.

•• Quick Chilli Con Carne

serves 1

small onion
small green pepper
cooking oil
125 g (4 oz) mince
seasoning
¼ × 5 ml sp (¼ tsp) chilli powder
small tin of baked beans

1 Chop onion and green pepper, fry in oil until soft, add mince, seasoning and chilli powder.

2 Allow the mixture to simmer until mince is cooked. Then add baked beans and simmer for a further 5 minutes.

Serve with boiled rice.

•• Chilli Con Carne

serves 2

oven temperature 200°C (400°F) gas mark 6

350 g (¾ lb) mince
85 g (3 oz) red kidney beans
onion
peppers (optional)
chilli powder
salt and pepper
1 × 15 ml sp (1 tbsp) gravy powder
tomato purée

Method 1

1 Add cold water to the mince and the red kidney beans. Cook the mince for ½ hour with the sliced onion and red and green peppers, if included, adding the chilli powder, salt and pepper.

2 After ½ hour thicken with gravy powder, add tomato purée.

Serve with rice and a vegetable or salad.

Method 2

Alternatively, put all the ingredients and water in a casserole and cook this in the oven for an hour and thicken as above.

(The red kidney beans should previously be soaked overnight.)

●● Beef in Beer

serves 2

oven temperature 180°C (350°F) gas mark 4

350 g (¾ lb) casserole steak
flour
fat for frying
1 onion
2–3 carrots
1 can Guinness
seasoning and mixed herbs

1 Cut the meat into chunks, roll in flour and fry in a little fat until browned. Peel and chop the onion and add to meat, frying until soft.

2 Put into a casserole dish with the chopped carrots and Guinness and cook for 2–2½ hours. Add seasoning and water as necessary.

Serve with baked potatoes.

●● Beef Burgers

serves 1

small onion
115 g (4 oz) mince (2 beef burgers)
tomato purée
mixed herbs
seasoning
1 egg
flour

1 Dice onion finely, mix into the mince, add tomato purée, herbs, seasoning and beaten egg. Mix well.

2 Divide into portions and pat into shape—coat in flour.

3 Fry top and bottom of burgers to seal, reduce heat and fry gently for 15 minutes or until the meat is completely cooked.

Serve with salad or potatoes and vegetables.

●● Spaghetti Bolognaise

serves 2

225 g (8 oz) mince
fat for frying
2 medium sized onions (chopped)
1–2 large carrots (grated)
60–125 g (2–4 oz) mushrooms
1 tablespoon tomato purée
½ beef stock cube and 275 ml (½ pt) hot water
salt, pepper and garlic to taste
spaghetti

1 Quickly cook mince in a little fat in a saucepan. The meat should turn brown. Transfer to a dish.

2 Fry onions in covered pan until golden. Add grated carrot and cook 2–3 minutes in covered pan. Wash and slice mushrooms and add to onions and carrots.

3 Return mince to pan add beef stock, tomato purée and seasoning to taste. Simmer gently for 20 minutes, stirring occasionally. Thicken with cornflour if desired.

4 Cook spaghetti as directed on packet. Strain and arrange on a plate or dish. Add bolognaise sauce.

●● Carbonade of Beef

serves 2

oven temperature 180°C (350°F) gas mark 4

225 g (8 oz) braising steak
30 g (1 oz) butter
2 medium sized onions
1 beef stock cube and 150 ml (¼ pt) hot water
1 can beer (small)
salt, pepper, garlic, herbs to taste

1 Wash steak and cut up into ½–1 inch cubes. Fry quickly in a saucepan with butter to 'seize' cubes. The meat will turn brown. Remove from pan and place in a dish.

2 Chop onions and fry gently until golden. Dissolve the stock cube in a little hot water and add to pan. Add can of beer. Season to taste.

3 Add the meat to the stock and place in a casserole dish in a moderate oven for 1–1½ hours. Thicken as desired with cornflour.

Serve with jacket or baked potatoes, peas, sprouts, etc.

(Alternatively, cook on the top of the cooker, simmer gently for 1 hour until meat is cooked and tender.)

Jugged Hare. Take hare and put in jug.

••• Pasta al Forno

serves 4

oven temperature 150°C (300°F) gas mark 2

1 onion
450 g (1 lb) minced beef
25 g (1 oz) lard
1 small tin tomatoes
salt and pepper
1 × 5 ml sp (1 tsp) mixed herbs
225 g (8 oz) pasta shells or similar
45 g (1½ oz) margarine
45 g (1½ oz) plain flour
425 ml (¾ pt) milk
175 g (6 oz) grated cheese

1 Fry the chopped onion and mince in the lard. Break up the tomatoes and add to the mince along with seasoning and herbs. Simmer for ½ hour.

2 Cook the pasta for 10 to 15 minutes in boiling salted water. Make white sauce (as for 'Cheese, Bacon and Potato Hotpot'), and add half the cheese to it.

3 Place half of the pasta in a well buttered casserole dish and cover with half of the cheese sauce and half of the mince mixture. Repeat with the remaining pasta, cheese sauce and mince. Sprinkle the remaining cheese over the top and bake for about 30 minutes.

Lamb

● Smothered Chops

serves 2

oven temperature 200°C (400°F) gas mark 6

2 lamb chops
1 onion
salt and pepper
125 g (4 oz) mushrooms
1 medium tin tomatoes

1 Place chops in a casserole dish. Peel onion, slice into rings and put on top of chops. Season.

2 Wash or peel mushrooms and add to dish. Pour over tomatoes and their juice.

3 Cover dish and cook for 1 hour near bottom of oven.

●● Lamb Anna

serves 2

oven temperature 200°C (400°F) gas mark 7

225 g (8 oz) stewing lamb
1 medium sized tin of butter beans
125 g (4 oz) small frankfurter sausages
thyme
salt and pepper
gravy powder or cornflour

1 Chop the lamb into smallish pieces, put in a casserole and add some water. Empty tin of butter beans over the meat. Slice the frankfurter sausages into 2 or 3 sections and put them into the casserole. Sprinkle with thyme, and add salt and pepper to taste.

2 Cook in a hot oven for one hour. Thicken with 1×5 ml sp (1 tsp) gravy powder or cornflour, mixed with a little cold water.

Serve with hot vegetables and potatoes. (Baked potatoes: put in oven with the casserole.)

•• Lamb Stew

serves 2

225 g (8 oz) stewing lamb (or other meat)
fat for frying
onion
carrots
parsnips (optional)
potatoes
beef stock cube and hot water
salt and pepper to taste
cornflour (if necessary)

1 Remove lamb from bone and cut up into bite-sized pieces. Fry quickly in a little fat in a saucepan until meat turns brown. Remove from pan and put in a dish.

2 Chop onions and fry in pan until golden. Peel and slice carrots, add to onions and cook with lid on. (Parsnips may be added with carrots if desired.) Peel and chop potatoes into bite-sized chunks.

3 Make up 575 ml (1 pt) stock and add to pan. Put in lamb and potatoes. Add salt and pepper. Simmer gently for 1 hour or until meat is tender and potatoes and carrots, etc. are cooked. The stew should be thick enough as the potatoes will tend to thicken it; if not, use a little cornflour mixed in cold water.

Serve in a dish with a slice of bread and butter.

Pork

- ## Pork Surprise

serves 2

oven temperature 200°C (400°F) gas mark 6

2 pork chops
mustard
60 g (2 oz) soft brown sugar
150 ml (¼ pt) milk

1 Pre-heat the oven to 200°C. Coat one side of the chops with mustard and press on the brown sugar.

2 Place the chops in an oven proof dish and similarly coat the top with mustard and sugar. Pour in milk to half way up the side of the chops and bake in the oven for 10 minutes.

3 Reduce the heat to 150°C (300°F), gas mark 2, and cook for a further 45 minutes.

Serve with green vegetables and boiled potatoes.

●● Wessex Casserole

serves 4

oven temperature 180°C (350°F) gas mark 4

4 slices of belly pork
3 cooking apples
3 medium potatoes
1 large onion
2–3 tomatoes (if available)
1 medium tin baked beans
salt and pepper
1 chicken stock cube

1 De-rind the pork and cut into cubes. Peel and slice the apples and potatoes. Peel the onion and chop finely. Slice the tomatoes.

2 Place the meat, vegetables and beans in a casserole dish in layers, season well and top with sliced potatoes.

3 Crumble the stock cube into some water and half fill the casserole dish. Cover and cook for about two hours removing the lid for the last 40 minutes.

●● Pork Chop and Cider Sauce

serves 1

1 pork chop
1 apple
1 small onion
butter
2 tsp plain flour
cider
salt and pepper

1 Wash the chop and place under grill. Turn (preferably more than once) so that both sides are brown.

2 Chop up apple and onion and fry together in butter until soft. Add 2 tsp of plain flour and heat for approx. ½ minute. Add cider to give a thickish gravy. Cook for 2 minutes and add salt and pepper to taste.

Serve with boiled potatoes and green vegetables or carrots, covering the chop with the sauce.

•• Pork and Bean Casserole

serves 2

oven temperature 200°C (400°F) gas mark 6

350 g (12 oz) belly pork or any cheap cut of pork
medium tin of baked beans
soy sauce
salt and pepper
1 × 5 ml sp (1 tsp) gravy powder

1 Chop the pork into pieces, put it in a casserole dish with the baked beans and add 4 × 15 ml sp (4 tbsp) water. Add soy sauce to taste, plus salt and pepper.

2 Cook at 200°C (400°F) for one hour, then thicken with gravy powder mixed with a little cold water.

3 Return to oven until gravy starts to simmer.

Serve with hot vegetables and potatoes.

•• Pork Casserole

serves 2

oven temperature 180°C (350°F) gas mark 4

2 pork chops or pieces of breast pork
fat for frying
1 large onion
salt and pepper
mixed herbs
1 tin baked beans
2–4 large carrots
1 tin tomatoes
1 glass cider
2 eating apples
1 × 5 ml sp (1 tsp) cornflour mixed with a little cold water

1 Cut up pork, fry with onion, add herbs and seasoning.

2 Place in a casserole dish, add beans, peeled chopped carrots, tomatoes and cider and peeled chopped apples. Stir.

3 Cover and cook in oven for 1–2 hours or until carrots are cooked.

4 Thicken with cornflour just before serving.

Serve with rice or baked potatoes which can be cooked along with the casserole.

••• Pork Chop Ardenaise

serves 1

1 small onion
fat for frying
1 pork chop
6 ½-cm (¼ in) pieces of bacon (ends of rashers)
2 × 15 ml sp (2 tbsp) cider vinegar or white wine
salt, pepper and herbs to taste
1 × 5 ml sp (1 tsp) cornflour
200 ml (⅓ pt) milk

1 Chop the onion and fry quickly in a little oil in a frying pan. Wash the pork chop and place in frying pan with the onions and quickly cook on both sides to seal in the juices—the chop will turn whitish. Turn the heat down, and add just enough water to the pan to cover the bottom and stop the chop and onions burning.

2 Add the bacon to this. Pour 1 × 15 ml sp (1 tbsp) of the cider vinegar or white wine onto one side of the chop. Allow everything to simmer gently for 5 minutes. Keep adding water if it is likely to boil dry. Add salt, pepper and herbs.

3 Turn the chop and put the other tbsp of vinegar/wine onto the other side of the chop. Simmer gently for up to 15 minutes or until the chop is cooked. Stir occasionally and add water as necessary.

4 Put 1 heaped tsp of cornflour into a cup and mix with the cold milk. Keep this on one side until you are ready to serve the meal.

5 When the vegetables are ready and the chop cooked, serve on a heated plate. After taking the chop from the frying pan, but leaving the onions and bacon, add the milk and cornflour and bring to the boil quickly to thicken. This will make a delicious cream white sauce which can then be poured over the chop and potatoes before eating.

Serve with vegetables and potatoes.

Sausages

- ## Lumberjack Pie

serves 1

oven temperature 190°C (375°F) gas mark 5

1 onion
1 small tin spam or luncheon meat
1 small tin baked beans
1 serving mashed potato (or make up instant)
knob of butter
salt and pepper
25 g (1 oz) grated cheese

1 Peel onion and chop finely. Cut spam into small cubes and place in an ovenproof dish with the onion. Cover with baked beans.

2 Mashed potato (or make up instant) with butter and seasoning and spread on top of mixture. Bake in oven for 30 minutes.

3 Sprinkle cheese on top and brown under a hot grill.

- ## Sausage Casserole

serves 2

oven temperature 170°C (325°F) gas mark 3

350 g (¾ lb) sausage meat
3 potatoes
2 tomatoes
125 g (4 oz) cheese

1 Put some water in the casserole dish and add the sausage meat. Slice the potatoes and lay over the sausagemeat (which should cover the bottom of the dish). Slice tomatoes and lay on the potatoes. Grate the cheese and sprinkle on top.

2 Cook for 1½ hours in a moderate oven.

Very good for an all-in-one hearty meal on a cold day.

• Sausage and Potato Supper

serves 1

oven temperature 190°C (375°F) gas mark 4

1 rasher of bacon (chopped)
125 g (4 oz) chipolata sausages
1 medium potato peeled and thinly sliced
1 small onion
15 g (½ oz) butter
seasoning
1 × 5 ml sp (1 tsp) mixed herbs
30 g (1 oz) grated cheese
150 ml (¼ pt) milk

1 Brown the sausages and bacon quickly under the grill. Chop the sausages into slices.

2 Arrange potato slices, onions, bacon and sausages in layers in a greased oven proof dish, sprinkling each layer with butter, seasoning and herbs. Finish with a layer of potato.

3 Cover with cheese, pour in milk and bake for 1 hour until potatoes are tender.

•• Sausage Burgers

serves 1

1 onion
125 g (4 oz) sausage meat
salt and pepper
mixed herbs (optional)
1 egg
1 × 15 ml sp (1 tbsp) flour
knob of butter or small amount of oil

1 Peel and chop onion finely. Mix the onion and sausage meat together in a bowl. Add seasoning and mixed herbs if used.

2 Beat the egg lightly and add to mixture to bind. Mix well. Form into balls, roll in the flour, and flatten with the palm of the hand.

3 Melt the butter or heat the oil in a frying pan, and cook the burgers for approximately 10 minutes on each side, or until brown.

●● Toad in the Hole

serves 2

oven temperature 200°C (400°F) gas mark 6

little lard
4 pork sausages
60 g (2 oz) plain flour
pinch salt and pepper
1 egg
little milk

1 Melt lard in an ovenproof dish in the hot oven. Prick the sausages and cook in the oven for 10 minutes turning once.

2 Put the flour, salt and pepper into a bowl making a well in the centre. Add the egg, beat until smooth, adding milk as it thickens.

3 Pour the batter over the browned sausages. Cook for 30–40 minutes. Serve when the batter has risen and browned.

•• Sausage and Rice Supper

serves 1

½ onion
little butter or oil
2 pork sausages
2 × 15 ml (2 tbsp) long grain rice
2 × 15 ml (2 tbsp) mixed vegetables
2–3 tinned tomatoes (or skinned fresh ones and a little water)
1 × 5 ml sp (1 tsp) mixed herbs
1 beef stock cube
425 ml (¾ pt) approx. hot water
salt and pepper

1 Chop onion, fry gently in the melted butter or hot oil until soft. Add sausages and cook until nicely browned.
2 Add rice and mixed vegetables and stir thoroughly. Add tomatoes, mixed herbs and stock cube dissolved in water.
3 Cook gently, stirring occasionally, for 30 minutes or until rice is cooked. Season to taste.
   N.B. Amount of water will vary according to how much rice absorbs. If mixture is too dry before rice is cooked, add more water. If too wet, cook for a few minutes extra.

•• Curried Sausage Savoury

serves 1

60 g (2 oz) sausages
1 small onion (chopped)
1 × 15 ml sp (1 tbsp) oil
60 g (2 oz) rice
1–2 tsp curry powder
salt and pepper
150 ml (¼ pt) chicken stock (made with stock cube)
60 g (2 oz) mushrooms (sliced)

1 Fry sausages and onions in oil until sausages are golden and onion transparent.
2 Add rice, stirring all the time with a wooden spoon, cook until translucent, then add curry powder, seasoning and stock. Cover and simmer on a low heat for 15 minutes.
3 Add mushrooms and continue cooking until all the liquid is absorbed and rice is soft.
   Serve with vegetables.

●●● Sausage Goulash

serves 1

125 g (4 oz) sausages
1 × 15 ml sp (1 tbsp) oil
1 small onion (chopped)
1 × 5 ml sp (1 tsp) paprika
1 × 5 ml sp (1 tsp) flour
small tin of tomatoes
150 ml (¼ pt) stock
pinch of thyme
salt and pepper
1 × 5 ml sp (1 tsp) tomato purée (optional)
½ a green pepper (chopped)

1 Grill sausages until brown.

2 Heat the oil in a frying pan and gently fry the onion until transparent. Then add the paprika and flour and stir. Cook for 1 minute.

3 Add the tomatoes, stock, thyme, salt and pepper, and tomato purée if used. Cut up sausages into approximately 2½ cm (1 inch) lengths. Add to the mixture in the frying pan and cook for 15 minutes before adding the green pepper and cook for a further 15 minutes.

Serve with potatoes or rice and a vegetable.

Offal

● Liver and Bacon Casserole

serves 2

oven temperature 180°C (350°F) gas mark 4

225 g (8 oz) lamb's or pig's liver
125 g (4 oz) streaky bacon
fat for frying
2 onions
tinned tomatoes
1 × 15 ml sp (1 tbsp) worcester sauce
chopped parsley

1 Cut up liver and bacon, fry for 5 minutes with the chopped onion.
2 Put into a casserole dish and add tinned tomatoes and worcester sauce. Cook for 1½–2 hours adding more water if required.
3 When cooked sprinkle with chopped parsley—gives a professional finish.

Best served with mashed potatoes.

●● Quick Faggots

serves 4

oven temperature 220°C (425°F) gas mark 7

225 g (½ lb) pigs liver
2 onions
225 g (½ lb) pork sausage meat
225 g (½ lb) breadcrumbs
1 × 5 ml sp (1 tsp) dried sage
½ × 5 ml sp (½ tsp) mixed herbs
salt and pepper
85 g (3 oz) suet or dripping

1 Chop the liver finely, peel and chop the onion. Mix the liver, onions and sausage meat.
2 Add the breadcrumbs, herbs and seasoning, suet or melted dripping; shape into 8 balls and pack closely into an oven-proof dish. Bake for 30 minutes.

Serve hot with gravy or cold with salad.

●●● Liver with Orange

serves 1

115–170 g (4–6 oz) pigs liver
1 medium sized onion (chopped)
fat for frying
½ beef stock cube and 150–275 ml (¼–½ pt) water
1–2 15 ml sp (1–2 tbsp) rice (long grain)
15 g (½ oz) butter or margarine
1 chicken stock cube and 575 ml (1 pt) water
1 medium orange
sugar

1 Gently fry liver and onions in a pan and add the beef stock. Cover and simmer gently for 20 minutes.

2 Fry the rice in the butter in another pan until the grains are white to golden brown. Gradually add the chicken stock, allowing the rice to swell and absorb more and more stock. Keep adding stock and water until the rice is soft. This should take the same time as the liver.

3 When the liver and rice are cooked, slice the orange into ½-cm (¼-in) slices and coat with sugar. Fry these gently in the pan with the liver until browned on both sides.

Serve the orange slices with the liver and sauce on a bed of the golden rice.

••• Kidneys Garibaldi

serves 1

2–3 lambs kidneys
knob of butter
1 medium sized onion
garlic to taste
½ sliced green or red pepper
4–5 button mushrooms
2 tinned tomatoes or 1 × 15 ml sp (1 tbsp) tomato purée
½ beef stock cube dissolved in 150 ml (¼ pt) water
salt and pepper
herbs and bayleaf to taste
cornflour

1 Slice the kidneys in half and remove the white core. Cut into 1 cm (½ in) pieces. Gently fry the kidneys in the butter in a saucepan until they are 'seized'. Remove from pan and place into a dish for later.

2 Chop the onion, garlic and pepper and fry gently in the pan until golden brown. Add the mushrooms, tomatoes or purée, stock and seasoning.

3 Replace kidneys and juices in pan and simmer gently for about 20 minutes. Thicken as necessary with cornflour.

The Kidneys Garibaldi are best served with rice, but boiled potatoes, spaghetti, etc. may be used.

Desserts

• Grilled Oranges

serves 2

1 large orange
2 × 5 ml sp (2 tsp) soft brown sugar
2 × 15 ml sp (2 tbsp) hazelnut yoghurt

1 Cut the orange in half crosswise. Cut around each half between the flesh and the skin, and between the segments.
2 Sprinkle the sugar on to the cut surface of the orange halves and grill them under a moderately hot grill for 5 minutes, or until the sugar is crisp.
3 Top each half with the yoghurt and grill for a further minute.

• Baked Apple

serves 1

oven temperature 180°C (350°F) gas mark 4

1 large cooking apple
2 × 15 ml sp (2 tbsp) jam, honey or syrup
mixed spice (optional)

1 Wash the apple and remove the core carefully. Place in a small dish.
2 Spoon the jam, honey or syrup into the hole in the centre, and put some in the bottom of the dish with a little hot water. Sprinkle with the spice, if used.
3 Cover with foil and bake for 1 hour or until the apple is soft.

● Toffee Apple Crisp

serves 1

125 g (4 oz) cooked stewed apple or apple purée
1 × 5 ml sp (1 tsp) Golden Syrup
15 g (½ oz) butter
1 × 5 ml sp (1 tsp) sugar
1 × 15 ml sp (1 tbsp) cornflakes (heaped)

1 Spoon the apple into an individual serving dish.

2 Melt the syrup and butter together in a pan, add the sugar and stir until dissolved. Stir in the cornflakes.

3 Spread the mixture quickly over the apple. Chill thoroughly before serving.

● Trifle

serves 4

1 packet trifle sponges
1 packet jelly (e.g. raspberry, tangerine, etc.)
sherry (optional)
1 packet custard powder
2 × 15 ml sp (2 tbsp) sugar
575 ml (1 pt) milk

1 Break the sponges into 2 and place in the bottom of a serving bowl. Make the jelly as directed and pour over the sponges. Add sherry if desired. Leave to set.

2 Make the custard as directed on the packet and pour over the jelly. Leave in a cool place for 2 hours.

Black Forest Gateau. Alternating layers of beech, cream, pine, etc. Garnish with leaves.

• Jelly Mousse

serves 3 to 4

1 packet jelly (any flavour)
275 ml (½ pt) water
1 small tin unsweetened evaporated milk

1 Make the jelly according to the instructions on the packet, but using only 275 ml (½ pt) of water. Leave in a cool place until almost set. Whisk well until the jelly is fluffy.

2 Add the evaporated milk and whisk again until the mixture is full of bubbles.

3 Pour into a basin and leave to set in a cool place. Chill before serving.

• Egg Custard

serves 4

oven temperature 140°C (275°F) gas mark 1

575 ml (1 pt) milk
2 eggs
2 × 15 ml sp (2 tbsp) sugar
knob of butter
nutmeg

Heat the milk almost to boiling. Beat the sugar and eggs together thoroughly. Pour on the hot milk stirring all the time. Pour into an oven proof dish. Add the knob of butter, and sprinkle with nutmeg. Bake for 45 minutes to 1 hour, or until set.

Serve warm or cold.

● Bread and Butter Pudding

serves 2

oven temperature 180°C (350°F) gas mark 4

2 slices bread (stale may be used)
25 g (1 oz) butter
few sultanas
2 × 15 ml sp (2 tbsp) sugar
1 egg
275 ml (½ pt) milk
mixed spice

1 Spread the bread with the butter and cut into small squares. Arrange in layers in a small ovenproof dish, sprinkling sultanas and sugar on to each layer.

2 Beat the egg, milk and mixed spice together, and pour over the bread. Leave to soak for 1 hour.

3 Bake in the oven for 30 minutes or until set.

● Rice Pudding

serves 3

oven temperature 150°C (300°F) gas mark 2

575 ml (1 pt) milk
85 g (3 oz) pudding rice or ground rice
60 g (2 oz) sugar

1 Warm the milk without boiling it.

2 Add the rice and sugar and pour the mixture into a greased dish and cook in a slow oven for 1½–2 hours.

Milk Sheik. Mix 1 pt of milk and quart of Duckhams 20/50 and chill.

● Pancakes

serves 4

125 g (4 oz) flour
2 eggs
salt
275 ml (½ pt) milk

1 Put flour in bowl, make a well in the centre and add the eggs and a large pinch of salt. Mix well, starting in the centre and gradually drawing in the flour. Add milk when the mixture becomes thick. Then add the rest of the milk and mix thoroughly.

2 Put small amount of oil into a pan and heat. Pour sufficient batter into the pan to give a thin layer, tilting the pan to ensure it covers the base. Toss when set (cowards can turn with a spatula!).

Serve with sugar and lemon juice, warmed jam, or fruit.

Variations
Make savoury pancakes with cheese, ham, mushrooms, cottage cheese, sweetcorn, etc.

● Birchermüsli

serves 4

fruit (e.g. grapefruit, pineapple, oranges, apples, pears, raspberries, strawberries, etc.)
285 g (10 oz) sweetened yoghurt or natural yoghurt
sugar to taste
1 lemon
85 g (3 oz) 'Familia' Birchermüsli powder, or Alpen, etc.
single cream or top of milk

1 Chop the fruit into small pieces. Put in a mixing bowl; pour in the yoghurt, add some single cream or top of bottle of milk; add the juice of the lemon and the Alpen (or substitute).

2 Mix well and put in a serving dish or bowls and decorate top with pieces of banana.

•• Apple and Ginger Crunch

serves 2

450 g (1 lb) cooking apples
2×15 ml sp (2 tbsp) water
50 g (2 oz) brown sugar
1×5 ml sp (1 tsp) grated lemon zest
225 g (8 oz) ginger biscuits

1 Peel and chop the apples, and cook in the water in a pan for approximately 10 minutes or until soft. Beat to a smooth purée with a wooden spoon, or rub through a sieve. Add the sugar, and lemon zest. Allow to cool.

2 Put the biscuits in a plastic bag and beat with a rolling pin to crush them.

3 Arrange layers of apple and biscuits in a dish, beginning and ending with a layer of biscuit. Chill. Serve with custard or cream.

•• Apple Crumble

serves 2

oven temperature 190°C (375°F) gas mark 5

450 g (1 lb) cooking apples
2×15 ml sp (2 tbsp) sugar
1–2×15 ml sp (1–2 tbsp) water
125 g (4 oz) flour
50 g (2 oz) butter or margarine
50 g (2 oz) sugar

1 Peel and chop the apples, and place in an ovenproof dish with the sugar and water. Bake for approximately 15 minutes.

2 Meanwhile, rub the butter or margarine into the flour, until it resembles fine breadcrumbs. Add the sugar and mix well.

3 Sprinkle the crumble mixture on top of the apples and bake in the oven for 20–30 minutes, or until the top is crisp and golden.

Variations
Different fruits may be used instead of apple, e.g. rhubarb, plums, gooseberries, blackberries, cherries etc. Currants, sultanas or cloves may also be added.

●● Sherry Cream Log

serves 5

1–2 glasses sherry
1 carton whipping cream
1 packet chocolate fruit and nut cookies

1 Pour the sherry into a bowl. Whip the cream until it is thick but spreads easily, i.e. not too dry. Have a dinner plate handy to arrange the log on.

2 Dip each biscuit in turn into the sherry and spread a little cream onto the flat side. Stack each bisuit as you do it onto the plate so that they become sandwiched together in a log. (They go soggy very quickly so be careful when spreading the cream.)

3 When all the biscuits have been used (allow 5–6 per person) spread the remainder of the cream all over the log to cover the biscuits. Rough up the cream to give a better effect and decorate with grated chocolate, nuts and cherries if desired.

Refrigerate for an hour before serving. (The biscuits will become cakey with the sherry and cream and solidify in the fridge.)

This makes a lovely quick and rich dessert to follow even the most ambitious meal.

●● Welsh Cakes

225 g (8 oz) self-raising flour
½ × 5 ml sp (½ tsp) salt
125 g (4 oz) butter or margarine
50 g (2 oz) sugar
125 g (4 oz) raisins or sultanas
150 ml (¼ pt) milk

1 Sift the flour and salt into a bowl, and rub in the fat. Add the sugar and fruit, and stir in the milk to bind.

2 Roll out on a lightly floured surface to a thickness of 1 cm (½ in) and cut into shapes with a pastry cutter.

3 Heat a little oil in a frying pan and fry the cakes gently, turning once, until brown on both sides.

●● Shortbread

oven temperature 150°C (300°F) gas mark 2
125 g (4 oz) butter
50 g (2 oz) sugar
175 g (6 oz) plain flour

1 Cream the butter and sugar together until soft and light. Add the flour and blend, then knead lightly to form a ball.

2 Roll out carefully on a lightly floured surface and cut into shapes with a pastry cutter.

3 Place on a greased baking sheet and bake for 20 minutes. Cool on a wire rack and dust with castor sugar.

●● Rice Cream Connaught

serves 5

½ an orange jelly
150 ml (¼ pt) water
575 ml (1 pt) milk
3 × 15 ml sp (3 tbsp) rice
1 × 15 ml sp (1 tbsp) sugar
2 × 15 ml sp (2 tbsp) orange squash
1 packet gelatine
1 large apple, pear or banana
1 small carton of cream

1 Melt the jelly in the water, pour it into a pudding basin and leave it to set.

2 Cook the rice gently in the milk, add the sugar and cool.

3 Melt the gelatine in the orange squash in a basin over a pan of hot water and add it to the rice mixture and allow to cool.

4 When the mixture begins to set, add the prepared fruit and carton of cream and pour the lot over the set jelly. When completely firm, stand the basin in hot water for 1 minute and turn out onto a plate.

●●● Apple Pie

serves 4

oven temperature 220°C (425°F) gas mark 7

450 g (1 lb) cooking apples
2×15 ml sp (2 tbsp) sugar
1–2×15 ml sp (1–2 tbsp) water
175 g (6 oz) plain flour
pinch salt
85 g (3 oz) butter or margarine
½–1×15 ml sp (½–1 tbsp) caster sugar
1½–2×15 ml sp (1½–2 tbsp) cold water

1 Peel and chop the apples and place in a shallow oven-proof dish, with sugar and water. Bake for about 15 minutes.

2 Meanwhile sieve the flour and salt, and rub in the fat until it resembles fine breadcrumbs. Add the caster sugar, then sprinkle on the water to bind the mixture. Form into a ball, but take care not to over handle. Roll out the dough on a lightly floured surface, and cut off a long narrow strip. Moisten the edges of the dish and press the pastry strip on to the rim. Then moisten this. Cover the apples with the remaining pastry, press the edges together and cut away the surplus pastry. Make a slit in the centre of the pie to allow steam to escape.

3 Bake for 30 minutes or until the pastry is cooked and golden.

Variations
Different fruits may be used, e.g. rhubarb, plums, gooseberries, blackcurrants, etc. Sultanas, currants or cloves may also be added.

Prune Charlotte. Take one Charlotte and cut off branches.

•• Victoria Sandwich

oven temperature 180°C (350°F) gas mark 4

125 g (4 oz) butter or margarine
125 g (4 oz) caster sugar
2 large eggs
125 g (4 oz) self-raising flour (or plain flour with 1 × 5 ml sp (1 tsp)
   baking powder)

1 Grease and flour two 17 cm (7 in) cake tins.

2 Using a wooden spoon, cream the butter and sugar until it is pale in colour, soft and fluffy. Beat the eggs lightly in a separate bowl and add gradually to the mixture, beating well between each addition. If the mixture shows signs of curdling (separating) add a little flour and mix well before adding any more egg. Sieve the flour (or plain flour and baking powder) and fold into the mixture, using a metal spoon.

3 Divide the mixture equally between the tins and smooth the surface. Bake in the centre of the oven for 15–20 minutes or until fim to the touch. Cool for 2–3 minutes in the tins, then turn out onto a rack.

4 When completely cold, sandwich together with jam or butter icing. Top with a sprinkling of icing sugar or caster sugar.

Butter Icing
125 g (4 oz) butter or margarine
225 g (8 oz) icing sugar

Cream the butter until soft, and gradually add the sieved icing sugar, mixing well.

Different flavourings can be added, e.g. grated lemon zest and a little lemon juice, grated orange zest and juice, cocoa powder or instant coffee powder dissolved in a little hot water, coffee essence etc.

Selections from the Trolley. Put wheels, bearings, etc. in dish and serve cold with ice cream.

Meal Suggestions

Those new to cooking may appreciate the following complete meal suggestions which are arranged in order of increasing difficulty:

1 Stewed steak, boiled potatoes, peas and carrots.
 Grilled oranges.

2 Pork surprise, creamed potatoes and green vegetables.
 Apple crumble.

3 Lamb stew, boiled potatoes and any vegetable.
 Fruit and yoghurt or cheese and biscuits.

4 Maison mince, creamed potatoes and green vegetables.
 Jelly mousse.

5 Liver and bacon casserole, baked potatoes and green vegetables.
 Fresh fruit topped with natural yoghurt.

6 Quick fish pie and green vegetables.
 Bread and butter pudding.

7 Pork chops and cider sauce, sauté potatoes, carrots or beans.
 Rice pudding.

8 Chilli con carne, rice and green salad.
 Jelly mousse.

9 Lamb anna, boiled potatoes and sprouts.
 Apple pie.

10 Sausage and rice supper.
 Apricot crumble.

11 Pizza and salad.
 Fresh fruit.

12 Pork and bean casserole, baked potatoes and cabbage.
 Fruit yoghurt.

13 Toad in the hole, baked potatoes and beans.
 Apple pie.

14 Cheese risotto.
 Fresh fruit.

15 Spaghetti bolognaise.
 Toffee apple crisp.

16 Devilled fish, rice and mixed vegetables.
Plum crumble.

17 Sausage goulash, sauté potatoes and cabbage.
Rice pudding.

18 Pork chop ardenaise, boiled potatoes and sprouts.
Apple and ginger crunch.

19 Kidney's garibaldi with rice.
Pear and peach crumble.

20 Pasta al forno and green salad.
Grilled oranges.

21 Chicken pie, boiled potatoes and beans.
Baked apple.

For Special Occasions

1 Vegetable soup.
Carbonade of beef, potatoes and a green vegetable.
Sherry cream log.

2 Quick onion soup.
Liver and orange, rice and green vegetables.
Baked apple with sultanas.

Harvey Headbanger. 8 vodkas, large cointreau, 1 bottle nail varnish remover and chilli powder to taste.

Salvage Techniques

1 *Sauces or stews with a lumpy sauce*

Remove the meat and any vegetables and keep them warm. Whisk the sauce sharply or rub through a sieve. Return the meat and vegetables and reheat.

2 *Sauce, soup or stew that is too salty*

Add a few slices of potato, simmer for 10 minutes then remove, or blend in a little milk or cream which absorbs the flavour.

3 *Sauce, soup or stew that is burned*

Do not stir—pour gently and carefully into a clean pan. If it still tastes burnt disguise the flavour with curry powder or mustard for a savoury dish, vanilla or almond essence for a sweet dish.

4 *Stew or casserole where the sauce is too thin*

Mix 1–2 × 5 ml sp (1–2 tsp) cornflour with cold water, add to the dish, stir thoroughly, and cook until thickened. Do not use flour as it will taste 'raw' unless cooked for 5–10 minutes.

5 *Pastry which sticks or breaks*

If the pastry is sticky, chill it in the fridge for 1 hour before trying again. If you do not have time for this, dust the board and rolling pin liberally with flour, but this lends to spoil the basic proportions. Alternatively, if the pastry breaks, roll between two sheets of greaseproof paper.

Glossary of Terms

1 *to dice:* using a sharp knife, cut into even-sized cubes.

2 *to poach:* to cook gently in liquid, e.g. water or milk.

3 *to simmer:* to cook just below boiling point.

4 *to seize:* to fry quickly over a high heat to seal in juices.

5 *to season:* to add salt and pepper.

6 *to cream:* using a wooden spoon, mix the ingredients (using fat and sugar) to the consistency of cream.

7 *to fold:* to incorporate flour usually into a cake mixture by flicking the ingredients gently together.

8 *to knead:* to work dough, pressing with the ball of the hand or knuckles, folding.

9 *to bake blind:* to bake, e.g. pastry case before the filling is added. Prick the base with a fork, and fill with either a crumpled sheet of cooking foil, or some rice, pasta or baking beans on a sheet of grease-proof paper, to prevent the pastry rising.

10 *zest:* the coloured part of lemon or orange peel—avoid the white part as it imparts a bitter taste.

11 *to scramble:* to stir egg mixture constantly with a fork.

12 *to sauté:* to fry lightly and quickly.

Acknowledgements

The editors wish to acknowledge the kindness and support of many people in the production of *The Campus Cookbook*. Primarily we are grateful to all those who have supplied recipes, especially to Delia Jones, who donated recipes from a previously unpublished cookery book, but also to Sheila Hockley, Tracy Outlaw, Sue Holti, Nicki Salmon, Wenda Cooper, Sian Brown, A. Pullen, Vicki Croudace, Margit Matthews, Kay Shaw, Paul Freeman, Jackie Willmott, Amanda, Adrienne Whitehouse, Les Antrobus and many others. Further, the book would not have been possible without the help and encouragement of Dorothy Richards, the design talent of Garry Denbury, and the support of many others including Richard Mawditt and Alan Baker. The drawings were by N. Senthilkuma.

DJL
HL

Index